The
Spanish Flu

**History of the Deadliest Plague
of 1918. Lessons to Learn and
Global Consequences of The
Great Influenza. Comparison
with the Pandemic of 2020 and
How to Prevent New Ones in
Future**

Arthur Franklin

Legal & Disclaimer

The information contained in this book and its
contents is not designed to replace or take the place
of any form of medical or professional advice; and
is not meant to replace the need for independent
medical, financial, legal or other professional advice
or services, as may be required. The content and
information in this book have been provided for
educational and entertainment purposes only.

The content and information contained in this book
has been compiled from sources deemed reliable,
and it is accurate to the best of the Author's
knowledge, information and belief. However, the
Author cannot guarantee its accuracy and validity
and cannot be held liable for any errors and/or
omissions. Further, changes are periodically made
to this book as and when needed. Where appropriate
and/or necessary, you must consult a professional
(including but not limited to your doctor, attorney,
financial advisor or such other professional advisor)

before using any of the suggested remedies, techniques, or information in this book.

Upon using the contents and information contained in this book, you agree to hold harmless the Author from and against any damages, costs, and expenses, including any legal fees potentially resulting from the application of any of the information provided by this book. This disclaimer applies to any loss, damages or injury caused by the use and application, whether directly or indirectly, of any advice or information presented, whether for breach of contract, tort, negligence, personal injury, criminal intent, or under any other cause of action.

You agree to accept all risks of using the information presented inside this book.

You agree that by continuing to read this book, where appropriate and/or necessary, you shall consult a professional (including but not limited to your doctor, attorney, or financial advisor or such other advisor as needed) before using any of the suggested remedies, techniques, or information in this book.

Table of Contents

INTRODUCTION - What Is the Flu?

Influenza, or flu, is a VIRUS. And this one attacks the respiratory system. **Attention!** The flu virus is highly contagious: When an infected person coughs, sneezes or talks, respiratory droplets are generated and transmitted into the air, and can then can be inhaled by anyone nearby.

Additionally, a person who touches something with the virus on it and then touches his or her mouth, eyes or nose can become infected.

Did you know?

During the flu pandemic of 1918, the New York City health commissioner tried to slow the transmission of the flu by ordering businesses to open and close on staggered shifts to avoid overcrowding on the subways.

The history of man, as well as that of animals, has been characterized by dozens of epidemics and pandemics caused by unknown viruses and others that we have come to know very well. In the last century, for example, the infamous Spanish flu of 1918 infected half a billion people, killing at least 50 million of them, although some estimates speak of 100 million deaths.

Most pandemics have an animal origin. That is, they are zoonoses.

In some cases, they arise from the close coexistence between people and farm animals and are then favored by large urban agglomerations with high population density. Other epidemics, however, have been determined by colonization and the conquest of new territories: viruses and bacteria unknown to the immune systems of indigenous peoples have caused real massacres.

One example is the period of the Spanish conquest in 16th century America, when smallpox killed almost three million Mesoamerican indigenous people and contributed much more than rifles and muskets to the invasion of the European conquistadors. Epidemics and pandemics have also been discussed in more recent times: an example concerns 2009 with influenza A / H1N1 (swine) and Sars-CoV-2, the cause of the Covid-19 pandemic.

But what exactly does pandemic mean? Can it be used as a synonym for an epidemic? It is worth trying to clarify some terms.

When a new or unknown virus comes into contact with humans, the results are almost never predictable. It may happen that it does not adapt to the new host at all, being controlled by the immune system and causing no harm. In these cases, those who come into contact with a pathogen may not even notice it.

In other cases, however, the virus manages to affect human cells (sometimes of a specific tissue, as in the latter case the lung), causing symptoms of various nature and severity: if we think about the ability of the virus to create damage to the our body, then we are thinking about its "pathogenicity".

Clearly, its most extreme form is represented by the patient's death: in these cases, we can evaluate the lethality of the virus, or the number of deaths out of the total number of patients who contracted that specific disease. The contagiousness or infectivity is quite another parameter. In this case, the terms are associated with the ability of the virus to spread from one individual to another: the more infectious a virus is, the faster it will spread within the population.

There is also a key value to understand this with concept, called $R0$: in epidemiology it is a numerical value that represents the average number of people who are infected by each infected person. If its value is 2, it means that each patient infects two healthy ones.

The higher the $R0$, the faster the pathogen spreads, while if this value is less than 1 the disease tends to extinguish itself in the population. $R0$ does not depend only on the characteristics of the infectious agent: population density and mobility, hygienic and climatic conditions and the number of immune or vaccinated people can limit or favor the spread of a virus.

When we want to take a picture of how quickly a virus is spreading, we can refer to terms such as endemic outbreak, epidemic and pandemic. An epidemic outbreak represents a well-defined community or region in which, in a certain period of time, there is a rapid increase in cases of a given infectious disease compared to what is expected.

The case of an endemic disease is different: in these cases, the virus is constantly present in the population and there can be a number of new cases that can increase or decrease over time, depending on the individuals susceptible to the disease. This is the case of measles in Italy, where in recent years the number of vaccinations has not been sufficient to guarantee adequate vaccination coverage. For this reason, over time, there have been times when the disease has recurred more frequently.

Finally, we speak of an epidemic when a pathogen spreads rapidly from a sick person to several people, increasing the number of cases of that disease in a defined geographical place, more quickly than normal.

An epidemic becomes a pandemic when, in addition to spreading from person to person and causing a significant number of deaths, it spreads globally. To declare a virus as a pandemic, it must comply with a classification with six progressive criteria developed by the World Health Organization: the final point is the ability to support growing epidemic outbreaks in two or more world regions.

Origin of the Pandemic Influence of 1918-1920

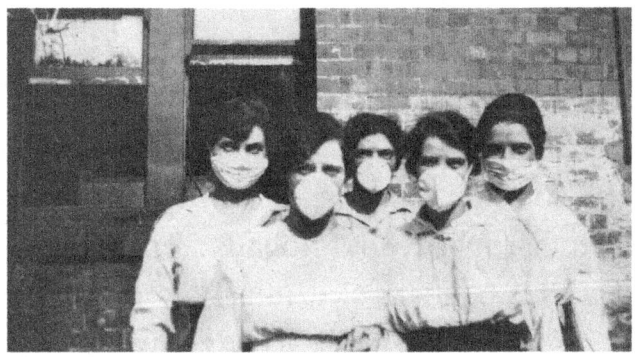

What we know as Spanish flu may actually have originated more than a century ago in the United States, in rural Haskell county in Kansas. Only later would it spread all over the world, mainly due to the troop movements caused by the First World War: it is the story taken up and told by the

American historian John Barry in The Great Influenza.

It is one of several theories on the presumed origin of the influence of 1918, on which, however, there will never be real certainty for the lack of sufficient historical-scientific documentation.

The epidemic, which probably caused over 50 million deaths, broke out in the spring of 1918, and then returned with great violence in the autumn. 60-70% of the deaths occurred in an incredibly short period of 14 or 15 weeks, between the end of September 1918 and the beginning of January 1919.

American soldiers destined for the European front were trained at home in extremely crowded fields, one of which was a few kilometres from the site of the virus's spread. Doctor Loring Miner was the first to notice this flu with strange symptoms and immediately alerted the authorities, but at that time the Wilson administration had other priorities and no one cared about what seemed to be just a modest local epidemic.

The military headquartered in the US training camps therefore began to become infected, but the symptoms were not yet serious enough to understand the extent of the disease and the troops were sent to Europe.

Two thirds of American soldiers heading to France arrived in Brest harbour, which was the first outbreak of infection in the old continent, while in the United States the epidemic developed starting from the army bases and from the ports where troops passed, such as Boston, Philadelphia and New Orleans.

The ships recorded dozens, sometimes hundreds of cases during the crossing: at that point the military health authorities understood the seriousness of the problem and tried to isolate the infected soldiers but it was now too late.

Why has this epidemic remained in history with Spanish?

For a very simple and at the same time disturbing reason: censorship. Spain was not at war at the time, so the newspapers were the first to talk about the first cases of death in rapid succession, describing the epidemic in its true dimensions.

TENS OF MILLIONS OF VICTIMS IN THE WORLD AT THE END OF THE WORLD WAR

The flu pandemic, which hit the world in 1918, is believed to be one of the greatest health disasters, for morbidity and mortality, that has plagued humanity in recent centuries. It is estimated that it infected around one billion people, killing between 21 and 25 million.

Other authors go to 40 million victims, considering that statistics in continents such as Asia, Africa and South America were not reliable and that the general health conditions were particularly precarious.

The fact that the scourge broke out in a limited period of time and at the end of the 1st world war, when the belligerent countries were exhausted and the military and civilian health organizations were in disastrous conditions, aggravated this event.

The epidemic was called at the Spanish time for a specific reason. Spain was immune from military censorship, as in Europe it was one of the few countries not involved in the war conflict, therefore health news, compared to the evolution of the epidemic in the Iberian country, was promptly provided by the press in the raw and dramatic reality.

This transparency, in the dissemination of health information, cost Spain the reputation of a nation where the epidemic was particularly virulent and the undeserved title of country source of contagion: which was not true.

The other states, engaged in the conflict, instead tried in every way to minimize the disclosure of epidemic data, operating with the censorship and self-censorship of the press.

It was believed that spreading dramatic news would weaken the morale of the populations and give the enemy strategic information on the recruitment capabilities of fresh troops to be engaged in the battlefields.

The problem of the origin of the pandemic of 1918 has been debated at length on a scientific level and the opinions are very different. It is not clear the extent of the first epidemic wave, which began in March, as it has not been definitively clarified if the spring viral strain had any relationship with the virus that broke out in late summer and, with dramatic effects, in autumn and during the winter of 1919.

At the beginning of the epidemic, during the spring phase, the health authorities did not require the reporting of cases of flu, as was later established from the United States when the second wave broke, therefore information on the beginnings of the different sub-epidemics are scarce and fragmentary.

As early as March, more than a thousand workers at the Ford Motor Company reported flu in the United States, but mortality was not noteworthy.

In the first days of March, the flu arrived in Kansas, at Camp Funston, a training base that housed 20,000 recruits.

In the same month of April, the flu affected over a dozen other military bases. In April the epidemic was reported in France, with the contagion of the troops.

Infections in the history of medicine

The name influence alludes to the punctuality with which the flu occurs every winter.

The medical term derives from the phrase "ab occulta coeli influentia" which began to be used in Italy in the seventeenth century, when the cause of the disease was attributed to the rigors of winter. The term flu already appears in 1580, when a 1386 flu epidemic is described.

As often happens in epidemics, other denominations were also recorded: it was called fièvre de Parme in France, of Flanders fever in England, of Bolshevik disease in Poland, of Bombay fever in Ceylon, of

Singapore fever in Penang, of soldier of Naples in Spain.

All this confusion in terminology arose from the diagnostic difficulty caused by the specificity of the symptoms, also common to other diseases.

At first the Franco-British territories and the civilian population; in June England and Italy were invaded, but at the same time China and Japan were affected in the east.

This first wave of high morbidity forced tens of miles of military personnel to bed and conditioned their operation. In the meantime, the Austro-German troops were also infected, enough to block the war efforts put in place to successfully end the war.

General Erich von Ludendorff, head of the German army, later went on to say that the influence had contributed to weakening the war offensive that the Central

Empires had unleashed in July, with the declared aim of winning the war.

Interesting is the importance of the incidence, among the Austrian soldiers and of the mortality which was almost triple compared to the Italian soldiers, this difference was mainly attributed to the fact that the soldiers of the Austro-Hungarian Empire were engaged on different fronts therefore exposed to more sources of contagion.

Another aspect to underline is that the food diet of the Austrians was based on meat, while that of the Italians was more vitaminic, based mainly on vegetables and fruit, therefore making the body more able to fight viruses.

When the second wave occurred in August, the lethal nature of the syndrome was added to the characteristic of high contagiousness.

From a demographic point of view, studies carried out later already showed that month unusually high mortality rates among young adults in the Indian sub-continent, in Southeast Asia, in Japan, in China, in most of the Caribbean, in large areas of South America and Central America.

In the United States, the second wave reached Boston on August 28, when a military ship carrying troops docked at the Commonwealth Pier. On that day 8 sailors fell ill, the following day 58, and on August 31 they were 81. On September 7 the soldiers hit rose to 119, but the first sick among civilians was also registered. The first three deaths were counted the next day: a military, a civilian and a Boston citizen.

Just in those days the epidemic touched Fort Devens, a military base 50 km from Boston, where 50,000 men were stationed and there, for the first time, it was perceived that this influence had characteristics that were beyond special.

In those days, a doctor from the Fort Devens base wrote a letter; this essay, found sixty years later in Detroit in a trunk, was published in the British Medical Journal. In this testimony the dramatic clinical picture with which the flu syndrome presented itself is described.

The disease began as a common flu, but when the patient entered the hospital immediately worsened due to acute pneumonia, cyanosis appeared, acute dyspnoea appeared in a short time and the exitus occurred due to suffocation. The doctor wrote that there were already 8 deaths a day since the beginning, but the figure tended to increase.

We know that 20% of the patients contracted the flu in a light form, the sick was massed in military hospitals and the health organization creaked under the pressure of the epidemic so much that they had to organize field hospitals to welcome the sick

In more serious patients, respiratory failure manifested itself acutely because the lungs were invaded by exudate, very high fever appeared, the patient got worse, lost in delirium, lost consciousness and died in a few days or in a few hours.

Other patients accused the common flu symptoms: chills, fever and myalgias, but on the fourth or fifth day the lungs were affected by a bacterial pneumonia that led to death or, in the most favourable cases, hesitated in a long convalescence.

Several epidemiologists have speculated that the Spanish virus spread by originating from the province of Kwangtung that originally this virus lodged in birds and that, thanks to genetic modifications, it was transmitted to pigs causing swine flu and then transferred to the man.

It has been hypothesized that it took about half a century for the transformation of the avian virus into human and that, at the end of this mutation, it became a lethal strain for human beings. This hypothesis would see the origin of the virus in southern China.

According to Kennedy Shortridge, Asia, and in particular southern China, is the epicentre of the flu epidemics. The virus is housed in birds, mainly ducks, raised in large numbers in this region.

A circuit would be created where ducks, pigs and humans come into play. Since the seventeenth century, Chinese farmers have found the opportunity to keep the rice fields free of weeds and insects thanks to the use of ducks.

As the rice grows, they leave the ducks in the submerged rice fields, which eat insects and weeds, but do not touch the rice.

When this begins to mature, they remove the ducks from the rice fields and move them to the canals and ponds. After the harvest, they reposition the ducks in the now dry rice fields.

Here the birds feed on the rice grains that have fallen to the ground, gaining weight considerably.

The zootechny of pigs is carried out in contiguity with the birds, so the passage of the flu virus to the pigs would take place and from these the adaptation of the virus towards man would be achieved through genetic modifications. In support of this thesis there would be evidence that influenza epidemics always seem to begin in that region of Asia corresponding to southern China.

According to this thesis, this benign evolution would be explained by the fact that in that remote and isolated area the population slowly immunized against this variant of avian virus. It remains unexplained that for several years this viral strain has remained in this geographical area without showing signs of itself in Asia or other continents.

Jeffery Taubenberger, an important molecular pathologist who studied biological material from deceased Spanish subjects and who sequenced parts of viral RNA from lung tissue of these patients, considers with scepticism the theory that sees the Chinese origin of the '18 pandemic.

His doubt is confirmed by the reading of a publication published in 1919 in the National Medical of China, where it is shown that in Harbin, one of the major cities of China, the epidemic showed exactly the same trend observed in the United States and Europe.

This article states that in the spring there was an initial wave of infections, caused by a very contagious, but not lethal virus, while in the autumn, when the second wave appeared, the lethality was very strong, affecting the Chinese, Europeans and the Americans.

Starting from this information, Taubenberger is of the opinion that in the spring the flu was already spread all over the world and there is therefore no evidence that the Spanish epidemic started in China rather than in the United States or Europe.

To understand the general climate that arose, the testimony of the medical colonel Victor C. Vaughan, a member of the Commission who visited the Devens Military Camp at the crucial stage of the epidemic, is of some interest.

In his memoirs, he reports that 66 men had died in the 24 hours before the visit and 63 died on the day of the arrival of the Commission. The hospital built for 2000 patients welcomed 8000. So, Vaughan said: hundreds of vigorous young men who with the American uniforms wearing them entered groups of 10 or more in hospital wards, where they were piled up on camp beds.

Soon they became cyanotic, and coughing they sputtered blood-veined mucus. In the morning the corpses were piled up in the morgue. Colonel Vaughan writes that at the autopsy table, the lungs of a young man who died in those days, appeared swollen and bluish, the surface was wet and foamy and their texture soft.

In North America the epidemic quickly spread to Massachusetts and out of this state to Vermont, the state of Maine and Toronto, Canada.

Nurses and doctors were missing, while the virus was rapidly spreading in military training camps and cities. In September, 12,000 Americans perished, mostly young people, and the training camps were quarantined.

It was therefore decided to revoke the recruitment of 142,000 men, despite pressing requests for troops from European battlefields.

In Philadelphia, the city that had paid a heavy tribute to yellow fever in the 19th century, men from the Navy were hit on 11 September.

Philadelphia was particularly battered, perhaps because a Liberty Loan Drive parade was held on September 20, with a crowd of 200,000 people.

In this situation, which was more worrying, on 18 September a campaign was launched in the country aimed at preventing people from coughing, spitting or sneezing in public places; from the 21st of the same month the flu became a disease to be reported.

This allowed to record the number of cases and therefore better follow the epidemic evolution.

The Origin and the Real

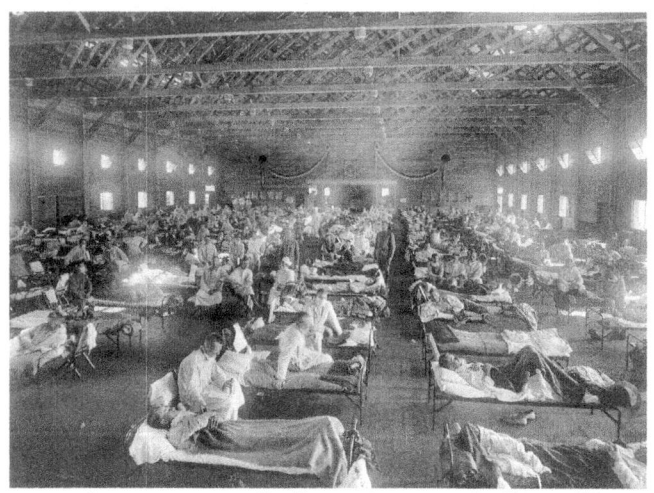

History of the Spanish Flu

La Spagnola: the great pandemic of 1918

In the final year of World War I, a virulent form of flu spread rapidly across the planet, becoming one of the deadliest events in history.

CONTEMPORARY AGE

WWI

In the summer of 1997, the scientist Johan Hultin went to Brevig Mission, an Alaskan town with a few hundred inhabitants. Hultin was looking for buried bodies, and the frozen soil of that region was the perfect place to find them. Digging into permafrost, he unearthed an Inuit woman who died nearly 80 years earlier, in excellent condition.

Biologists at St. Bartholomew's Hospital in London are analysing the brain and lung tissue of victims of the 1918 pandemic. Biologists from St. Bartholomew's Hospital in London are analysing the brain and lung tissue of victims of the 1918 pandemic.

With permission from the local authorities, the scientist took a sample from one of his lungs before he buried the woman. Brevig Mission was just one of many locations hit by a tragedy of global proportions, one of the worst that ever happened to humanity: the 1918-19 flu pandemic.

Known - improperly - by the name of Spanish influence, or simply Spanish, this epidemic spread with surprising speed all over the world, even bringing India to its knees and reaching Australia and the remote Pacific islands.

In just 18 months, the flu infected at least a third of the world's population. Estimates on the number of deaths vary enormously, from 20 to 50 or even 100 million victims.

If the higher figure were reliable, the 1918 pandemic would have killed more people than they killed the two world wars together.

Influences are caused by several types of closely related viruses, but one particular form (type A) is linked to lethal epidemics. The 1918-19 pandemic was caused by a flu virus of this type, called H1N1. Although it became famous under the name of Spanish influence, the first cases were registered in the United States during the last year of the First World War. In March 1918 the United States had been at war with Germany and the central empires for eleven months. As the whole nation mobilized for the conflict, fortified posts on US soil experienced massive expansion.

First aid to treat patients affected by the 1918 pandemic at the Camp Funston US training camp in Kansas, where the first official Spanish cases were recorded

One of these was Fort Riley, Kansas, where a new training camp was built to accommodate part of the 50,000 men who would be drafted into the army: Camp Funston. It was there that, on March 4, a soldier appeared feverish in the infirmary. Within a few hours, more than a hundred of his fellow soldiers showed symptoms of the same disease, and others would fall ill in the following weeks. In April, US troops arrived in Europe, bringing the virus with them. It was the first wave of the pandemic.

A lethal speed

The flu killed its victims with incredible speed. Stories abounded in the United States about people waking up sick and dying on the way to work. The symptoms were gruesome: patients had fever and difficulty breathing. Due to the lack of oxygen, their faces took on a bluish complexion. The bleeding filled the lungs with blood, causing vomiting and nose bleeding and eventually suffocating people in their fluids.

Like so many other flu forms before her, the Spaniard affected not only very young and very old people, but also healthy adults between 20 and 40 years of age. The main factor in the spread of the virus was, of course, the international conflict, which had reached its final stages at the time. Epidemiologists still argue about its exact origins today, but many agree that it was the result of a genetic mutation, possibly in China. It is clear, however, that this new form of flu spread globally thanks to the massive and rapid movement of troops around the world. The dramatic nature of the conflict also ended up masking the unusually high mortality rates of the new virus.

At first this kind of the disease was not understood and a lot of deaths were almost always attributed to some kind of pneumonia. Strict wartime censorship prevented the European and North American press from reporting epidemics. Only in neutral Spain could the newspapers speak freely about what was happening, and it was from the coverage that the media in that country gave it that the disease took its nickname.

The second wave

The trenches and overcrowded camps of the First World War became fertile ground for the disease.

When the troops moved, the contagion travelled with them.

Appearing for the first time in Kansas, the flu dropped in intensity within a few weeks, but it was a temporary respite. In September 1918 the epidemic was ready to enter its most lethal phase.

Seems that the period between September and December 1918, after the 13 was the most intense period, with a lot of deaths. In Italy the most aggressive phase occurred between July and October of that year, when even three thousand people per day fell ill.

Again, it was in the crowded military camps that the second wave initially took root. When the crisis peaked, health services began to fail.

Funeral directors and gravediggers were in difficulty and making individual funerals became impossible.

Many of the dead ended up in mass graves. The end of 1918 brought an interval, a small pause in the spread of the virus, and in January 1919 it starts the third and final phase.

By now the disease was decidedly less violent: the ferocity of the autumn and winter of the previous year did not repeat itself and the mortality rate dropped.

But the final wave still managed to cause considerable damage.

Australia, which had immediately imposed the quarantine obligation, managed to escape the most virulent effects until the beginning of 1919, when the disease also arrived there, causing the death of several thousand people.

However, for those who had lost loved ones or experienced long-term complications, its effects would have been felt for decades.

A lasting impact

The pandemic spared practically no part of the world. In Italy, according to the Central Statistical Institute, around 300,000 people died in 1918 alone.

In Britain 228 thousand people died; in the United States about half a million; in Japan 400 thousand. Western Samoa (now

Samoa) in the South Pacific lost 23.6 percent of the population.

The researchers estimate that, in India alone, deaths have reached a figure between 12 and 17 million.

Data on the number of deaths are vague, but in general it is estimated that mortality was between ten and twenty percent of those infected.

The samples taken in 1997 by Johan Hultin from the woman from Brevig Mission served to make scientists better understand how flu viruses change and spread.

Thanks to medicines and improved public hygiene - in addition to the presence of international institutions such as the World Health Organization - the international community is now very much in the face of the threat of a new epidemic.

What was exactly the Spanish Flu and Why the name "Spanish Flu"?

Spanish influence, why was it called like this?

May 29, 1919, Massachusetts. As in all countries, here too, following the filling of hospitals, field hospitals were built to meet the needs of the sick.

In the spring of 1918, 102 years ago, the whole world was hit by a flu disease that infected three thirds of the world's population in three different waves, causing over 50 million deaths.

In the middle of the First World War

The serious pandemic with its impressive load of victims could spread all over the world mainly because of the world war that had moved millions of soldiers, also coming from other continents, on the battlefields of Europe, wearing them out in a trench war in which promiscuity, malnutrition, poor hygiene, other infectious diseases and parasites also weakened young and healthy organisms.

The precarious conditions of overcrowding and lack of medicines in which the field hospitals that had to treat wounds from war and chemical attacks were found, contributed to aggravate the situation. Most of the deaths occurred from complications, i.e. from infections with other pathogens.

Why is it called "Spanish influence"?

But why is this influence known as Spanish? In reality Spain was not the place of origin, but it was the only country that broke the news. In fact, the Iberian country was not involved in the war conflict and therefore the news was not censored as it happened in the warring nations that feared the spread of panic.

What we should learn from the 1918 flu pandemic

The biggest lesson of the 1918 pandemic is clearly what people need to tell the truth, because not telling the truth causes people to underestimate the disease while today, in general, people can face the truth. It is the unknown that is much more frightening

Let's try to replace the new coronavirus with the Spanish flu epidemic, 1918 with 2020, and try to see the differences.

The 1918 flu killed between 50 and 100 million people worldwide.

"In 1918 there was a slight spring wave of flu that was underestimated and that returned in the autumn more virulent and deadly. Probably 60-70% of the deaths about 14 or 15 weeks, from late September to December, perhaps, in certain places, it lasted until January ".

The 1918 flu pandemic. - CBS

In that period the last months of the First World War were lived and more soldiers of influence died than from the clashes that took place on the battlefields during four years of fighting.

Unlike the new coronavirus, the most vulnerable to infection were twenty years old.

"The most horrible symptoms were bleeding that could occur not only from the nose and mouth, but also from the eyes and ears," says Barry. "Dark blue people for lack of oxygen due to breathing difficulties, the doctors found it difficult to distinguish white soldiers from African American soldiers".

It was called Spanish influence but only because Spain, which was not belligerent, allowed the press to report on it, which was not allowed by the censorship of the warring countries.

The first major outbreak in the United States occurred at Camp Funston (now Fort Riley) in Kansas. Infected soldiers were sent to the French front, allowing the virus to spread.

In the United States, the press was not allowed to talk about it.

A year earlier, President Woodrow Wilson had promulgated the Sedition Act, making it a crime to say or publish something negative that would affect the war effort.

Barry recounts: "Wilson created what was called the public information committee. The architect of that committee justified it by declaring that 'Truth and lies are arbitrary terms. The strength of an idea lies in its inspirational value. It matters little if this is true or false or".

"In the United States, there were national public health leaders saying things like 'This is ordinary flu by another name.' The same kind of thing was happening locally. "

With deadly consequences.

The Global issues and Effects of the Great Influenza, the Deadliest Plague in history

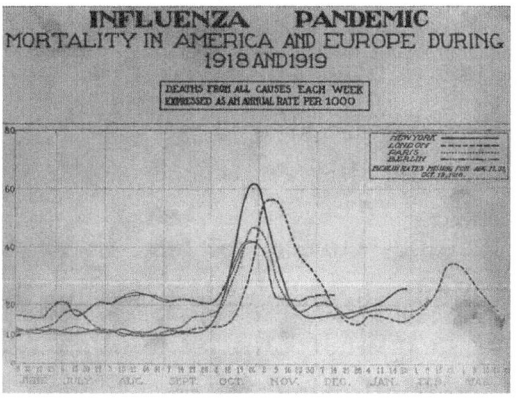

Spanish flu: symptoms and deaths of the largest pandemic in history

It suddenly appeared in the final stages of the First World War and in the following two years it claimed tens of millions of victims worldwide, disappearing in the same way it started.

When we talk about a pandemic, or an epidemic capable of affecting many parts of the world with a high number of cases and high mortality, the first thought often falls on the notorious black plague, which in 1300 killed 20 million people in Europe; however, the one that has claimed the most victims ever is the cryptic

Spanish flu or great flu, a disease that between 1918 and 1920 killed between 25 and 50 million people, after having infected about a billion of them. Recent estimates even speak of 100 million deaths.

The halo of mystery that surrounds the appearance, spread and disappearance of the "Spanish" is intimately connected to the period in which it emerged, or the final phase of the First World War. For reasons of censorship, in fact, the pandemic was kept hidden by various regimes in a large part of the world, at least in the first year of its onset.

The Spanish flu was, as the name suggests, an extremely virulent type of flu - carried by the H1N1 virus - and the largest pandemic in human history. The name "Spanish" derives from the fact that when it began to spread, the newspapers of the Iberian country mainly spoke of it, this was because Spain was not involved in the First World War and therefore freedom of the press was not subject to the limits of war censorship.

Moreover, announcing that a mysterious epidemic was mowing down population and soldiers could not have a positive impact on the morale of the troops, already worn out for years of hard trench warfare.

How it spread

Understanding when, where and how exactly the great influence emerged is quite complex, precisely because of the historical context in which it struck, however the documents indicate that the first recorded cases, in the winter and spring months of 1918, were not lethal, and the pathology it presented itself as a flu form that lasted a few days with no consequences whatsoever.

It was called the "three-day flu" and simply referred to as a strange disease. It was believed that the first outbreak was a fort in Kansas or another in Texas, where 1,100 soldiers were affected, but other research indicates a country in France and also Asia.

For the reasons already listed, Spain was also considered the theatre of the first outbreaks. In the summer of 1918, the flu erupted in all its virulence, accompanied by very serious lung complications that were responsible for most of the deaths. It is believed that in Europe it was introduced precisely by American soldiers, who landed in France in April 1917 to participate in the conflict. However, Spanish influence struck at all latitudes, even involving the Arctic and remote Pacific islands. Suddenly disappeared two years after the appearance, probably due to a mutation of the virus in a less lethal form, although some believe that the most effective treatments to combat pneumonia have had a significant impact.

The lethality of the virus

Despite being particularly aggressive, the flu was not directly responsible for the mortality rate: the deaths were in fact caused by bacterial infections that attacked the affected patients, often in extremely precarious hygiene and health conditions. Just think of the soldiers barricaded for years in the trenches, a veritable heap of viruses and bacteria that could thrive among corpses, animal carcasses and open sewers.

To avoid such a massacre antibiotic would have been enough, effective in counteracting complications of bacterial origin, however penicillin was discovered only ten years after the end of the conflict by Alexander Fleming.

The situation in Italy

Italy was one of those most affected by the Spanish influence; the mortality rate was second only to the Russian one, where extreme weather conditions further aggravated the situation. It is estimated that in Italy the disease affected over 4 and a half million people, killing between 375,000 and 650,000. An impressive number, considering that at the time the Italian population was made up of 36 million citizens. The flu hit mainly in the South, but mortality varied greatly from area to area, with peaks of 70 percent in some cities. Already tried by the war, Italy was brought to its knees also because among the dead there were many doctors and nurses, but also transport workers, that is, drivers, trams and railway workers, more exposed because in contact with a large number of people.

A massacre of young people

Although it may be thought that the greatest number of victims was concentrated in the most exposed age groups, i.e. children and the elderly, in reality the most affected were young people between 18 and 30 years. There are two opposing theories about it. As is known, virus strains are distinguished by the characteristics of two proteins, namely hemagglutinin (H) and neuraminate (N), hence the names H1N1, H3N2, H5N1 and so on, which have become sadly famous in association to the risks of avian influenza. Due to the appearance of viruses similar to that of the Spanish one (or of the form H1N1) in the early 1900s and before 1890, the subjects born in the "uncovered" time interval were the least protected by the

Spanish, since unlike the others had not developed immune defences. Others suggest that the cause may have been a so-called "cytokine storm" triggered by a disproportionate immune system reaction, more efficient in young adults.

The Spanish of 1918 and the responsibilities of science

The official estimates of the victims of the great flu pandemic of 1918, better known as "Spanish", amount to about 50 million deaths worldwide (675 thousand in the United States only). The reconstruction of the 1918 virus through the synthesis of all its eight subunits and the generation of the infectious virus itself is described in issue 5745 of the journal Science, published 7 October 2005. The sequences of the last three virus gene segments are instead illustrated. in an article published in the 437 issue of Nature of 6 October 2005.

As expected, the sequencing has fully revealed that it is a virus much more lethal than the "normal" flu strains. The result is therefore two news items, one good and one bad. The point then is: should the sequencing of the Spanish virus have been kept hidden or is it right to have made it available to the whole scientific community, despite the risks associated with bioterrorism?

This is a rather complex and delicate issue, which has been discussed at least since September 11, 2001. Moreover, the American Scientific Committee for Biosafety was set up precisely to offer specific advice to government agencies and the scientific community in on transparency and disclosure policies. It is reassuring to know that this body, when asked about the opportunity to publish the 1918 virus studies, expressed itself favourably, concluding that the benefits for science deriving from this information have an extremely greater value than the potential risks.

We are deeply convinced that publishing was the right decision, both in terms of national security and public health. Of course, it is impossible to predict how scientific observations will stimulate the discovery of new treatments or new procedures for the control and management of pandemics.

For example, in the Nature article, the comparison between the sequences suggests that the Spanish virus originated not from a series of changes in the polymerase genes, but from the movement of these genes, en bloc, from an avian source into an influenza virus human.

The availability of this information will allow the identification of the avian origin of the genetic material and will clarify why this particular set of genes has been selected. Similarly, the results of the Science article suggest that cutting a protein on the surface of the 1918 virus (a key step in triggering the infection) could result from a new mechanism.

A hypothesis that, if verified, could lead to the synthesis of new drugs capable of blocking this passage and thus preventing the outbreak of a pandemic.

People also need to know that the Spanish virus cannot leave research labs. In fact, all the experiments are carried out in biosecurity level 3 structures, as recommended by the American CDCs and the National Institutes of Health. Currently available data seem to suggest that some drugs and possible future vaccines will be able to counteract the infection caused by the Spanish virus.

Therefore, the recent political decision to stock large quantities of antivirals seems wise.

How USA government and people reacted

In the absence of clear data on the nature of the pandemic, the measures taken by the health and military authorities were simply symptomatic and empirical.

It was generally advised to air the rooms, avoid crowded places (theatres, cinemas and schools were closed), stay in bed, hydrate with hot liquids, put cold compresses on the head, wear protective gauze masks, etc.

The drugs used were: aspirin, adrenaline (for secondary pneumonia), subcutaneous oxygen, quinine salts, digitalis, isotonic solutions of glucose and sodium bicarbonate intravenously and even cinnamon.

Doctors advised soldiers to spray antiseptics and alcohol in their throats and chew tobacco to lower the temperature.

They also attempted to inoculate "vaccines" based on body secretions (blood and mucus) or bacteria believed to be responsible, filtered to eliminate larger cells and debris ", as reported by Alfred W. Crosby.

All these measures proved completely useless if not harmful: the vaccinated inevitably ended up getting sick and dying like flies, unlike the unvaccinated ...

Mortality was very high, at least 40%.

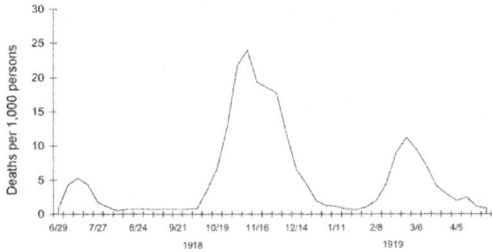

There are very few people who realize that the worst epidemic that has ever hit America, the so-called Spanish Flu of 1918, was caused by the massive vaccination campaign carried out across the US federation.

The doctors said to the population that this flue is caused by germs.

No one knows about the viruses at that time. Germs, bacteria and viruses, along with bacilli and a small number of other invisible organisms are the scapegoats on which doctors love to blame things they don't understand.

If a doctor makes a mistake in making a diagnosis and prescribing therapy, and kills his patient, he can always blame the germs, and claim that his patient's infection had not been previously diagnosed and therefore came to him. too late. If we go back to 1918, the period in which the flu exploded, we will notice how it exploded immediately after the end of the First World War when our soldiers were returning home from overseas.

This was the first war in which all the vaccines then known were compulsorily administered to all the military.

This hodgepodge of drug poisons and putrid proteins of which the vaccines were composed, caused such a spread of disease and death among soldiers that it was a common topic of discussion that our men were killed more by the injections of the doctors than by the bullets of firearms. Many were disabled and returned home or ended up in a military hospital, like hopeless wreckage, before they even saw a battlefield.

The percentage of illnesses and deaths among vaccinated soldiers was four times higher than for unvaccinated civilians. But that didn't stop the vaccine promoters. Vaccines have always been a big business, and so we persistently continued to use them.

It was a shorter war than the vaccine manufacturers had thought, it only lasted a year for us, and so the vaccine manufacturers were left with an amount of unused and spoiled vaccines that they wanted to sell for a good profit.

And so they did what they usually do, held a closed door meeting and planned the dirty program, a federal (worldwide) vaccination operation that would use all their vaccines, telling the population that the soldiers were returning home with many terrible diseases contracted in foreign countries and that it was a patriotic duty for every man, woman and child to protect themselves by running to the vaccination centres and giving all the injections.

The result was that almost the entire population underwent injections without being touched by doubt, and it was only a matter of hours before people began to agonize and die, while many others collapsed affected by diseases of such virulence that no one had never seen anything like this before.

These diseases had all the characteristics of the diseases against which people had been vaccinated, high fever, chills, pain, cramps, diarrhoea, etc. typhoid fever, throat and lung congestion similar to pneumonia and typical of diphtheria, vomiting, headache, weakness and torment of hepatitis caused by jungle fever vaccines, and the manifestation of sores on the skin caused by smallpox vaccines, along with paralysis caused by all vaccines, etc.

The doctors were disconcerted, and said that they didn't know the cause of this strange and deadly disease, and that they certainly had no cure.

They should have known that the hidden cause was vaccinations, because the same thing happened to the soldiers after receiving vaccination injections in the barracks. Vaccines for typhoid fever caused an even worse form of the disease, which they called para-typhoid.

So, they tried to suppress the symptoms of this disease with a stronger vaccine, which in turn caused an even more pernicious disease, which killed and disabled many men.

The combination of all those toxic vaccines that fermented together in the body caused such violent reactions that doctors were unable to deal with that situation. The disaster spread rapidly to the camps. Some military hospitals were filled exclusively with paralyzed soldiers, and were considered war injuries, even if they occurred before they left American soil.

Doctors did not want the spread of this disease caused by vaccines to backfire, and they agreed with each other to call it the Spanish flu. Spain was a faraway place, and some of the soldiers had been there, so the idea of calling it Spanish Influence seemed like a great choice to blame someone else.

The Spaniards resented the fact that this worldwide scourge had taken the denomination from them. They knew that the disease had not originated in their country. Twenty million people died worldwide of that flu epidemic and seemed to touch all the countries that were reached by vaccination.

Greece and a few other nations, which did not accept the vaccine, were the only ones not affected by the flu.

Doesn't this prove something? At home (in the USA) the situation was the same; the only ones who escaped the flu were those who refused vaccinations.

My family and I were among the few who persisted in rejecting the strong propaganda pressures, and none of us had the flu, not even a little cold, despite the fact that the sick was all around us, and in the in the middle of the coldest period of winter. Everyone seemed to have taken it.

The whole city was prostrate, all sick or dying. Hospitals were closed because doctors and nurses had been affected by the flu. Everything was closed, schools, offices, post offices, everything in short, nobody went on the street.

It was like a ghost town. There were no doctors to take care of the sick, and so my parents went from house to house doing everything possible to help people affected by the disease.

But germs weren't the cause of that or some other disease, and so they weren't affected. I talked to a few other people after that, who said they survived the 1918 flu, and so I asked them if they got vaccinated, and they all told me they never believed in the validity of the vaccines and that they didn't they hadn't made one.

Common sense shows us that all those toxic vaccines injected together in people could not help but cause heavy body poisoning, and poisoning of some kind is usually the cause of the disease.

The flu of 1918 was the most devastating we have ever faced, and in an attempt to eradicate it all the substances known in the medical paraphernalia were used; but the addition of these drugs, each of which represents a poison, did nothing but intensify the condition of hyper - poisoning of the sick, so that the treatment of the disease actually killed more than the flu itself did.

Vaccine Development in the USA

A dive into the past: the mask of Spanish fever

At the end of the First World War, around 50 million people died from the Spanish fever. Masks were the most popular line of defence for those who had not been infected.

Spanish fever patient zero may have been a WWI soldier who accidentally transported the virus and returned to the heavily packed military camp in Fort Riley, Kansas. From that moment, those who had contracted the disease would march through all the battlefields of Europe and beyond, taking it with them. A fifth of the world's population was infected with Spanish fever. An estimated 50 million people died from the disease worldwide, from isolated Arctic villages to remote Pacific islands, three times more people than the victims of the actual conflict.

When the pandemic spread from 1918 to 1920, doctors believed that fever was caused by bacteria. In any case, it wouldn't have made much difference if they had known from the outset that it was a virus, since antivirals did not yet exist and the fever vaccine had not yet been developed.

Access to theatres, churches and other public places indoors was forbidden, in some cases even for a whole year, for fear that bacteria could spread to so crowded places. Even the funeral was limited to 15 minutes.

As the first method of defence against the contraction and transmission of the disease, masks, usually made of fabric, were requested to be worn in public and access to trams, offices and other public spaces was forbidden if the mask was not worn.

When the mask didn't work, all possible alternatives were applied. The leaflets suggested chewing food carefully and avoiding wearing tight clothes and shoes, there was even a ban on coughing and sneezing in public.

Home remedies included gargle with baking soda and boric acid, salt packs in the nostrils and eating onions at all meals.

In the 1930s, it was discovered that the cause of the fever was a virus and not a bacterium. At the end of the decade, in 1938, Jonas Salk and Thomas Francis developed the first vaccine against fever viruses.

Nowadays, about half of the American population undergoes the flu shot.

According to Phil Dormitzer, vice president and scientific director of viral vaccines at Pfizer, one of the main challenges in the development of better flu vaccines is to "exploit the modern idea of immunity to create vaccines with a broad, effective, tolerable and adequate action, in so that everyone continues to undergo treatment every year. "

Additionally, in recent years, an aspect of Spanish fever has returned to the surface for beneficial purposes: researchers have tested the blood of epidemic survivors to find possible clues in the development of immunity against modern avian influenza incarnations.

Although the population of our planet has experienced several pandemics caused by viruses in the last century, one of the pandemics recognized as one of the worst was undoubtedly the "Spanish" flu of 1918.

But how much can this pandemic be shared? to the current one from SARS-CoV-2?

And what lessons can we learn from the flu epidemic which the last century decimated (along with the first war conflict) the population of the European continent and beyond? Here are the similarities and differences between the Spanish flu and the new corona virus.

Although in the last century the population of our planet has faced several pandemics caused by viruses, one of the pandemics recognized as one of the worst was, without doubt, the "Spanish" flu of 1918 (incorrectly so defined not as it was first arisen in the Iberian country, but because the first to talk about it were the Spanish newspapers, not subjected to the censorship of war prevailing in other European countries, which long hid the existence of a pandemic).

But how much can this pandemic share the current one from SARS-CoV-2?

And what lessons can we learn from the flu epidemic which the last century decimated (along with the first war conflict) the population of the European continent and beyond?

Here is a brief review of the similarities and differences between the two pandemics.

Viruses involved

Flu pandemic of 1918

It was caused by an avian-origin H1N1 flu virus. Research published in 2005 suggests that it originated in the US (and not in Spain). The virus responsible for that pandemic is believed to have infected 500 million people worldwide (equal to one third of the entire world population then).

According to some estimates, the pandemic caused 50 million deaths worldwide, with an estimated lethality of between 2% and 10% (seasonal flu has an average lethality rate of 0.1 %).

New Coronavirus Pandemic (SARS-CoV-2)

Informally known as Wuhan's coronavirus, from the name of the Chinese locality where the first outbreak of infection subsequently became pandemic, it is caused by SARS-CoV-2, a viral strain of the coronavirus subfamily.

It is the seventh virus that made the leap of animal-human species (in this case from a bat) and acquired the ability to infect people in an interhuman way.

The estimated global rate for new Coronavirus disease (Covid-19) would be close to 5% (2% in the US) although some experts believe this percentage to be underestimated due to the existence of doubts about the accuracy in reporting disease cases by the Chinese authorities, where the infection originated.

According to prof. Anthony Fauci, director of the US National Institute for Allergy and Infectious Diseases, currently with no face as an expert Task Force deputy to combat the pandemic in the United States, the case fatality rate is projected instead of around 1%, which is however 10 times the lethality rate of a typical seasonal flu.

Pneumonia is the common killer factor for both infections.

Many of the deaths ascribed to Covid-19 are linked to a particularly severe form of pneumonia, due to the weakening of the immune system, weakened by the fight against the virus. This feature is partly shared with the 1918 influenza pandemic (although there are differences in terms of lethality rate in favor of SARS-CoV-2-borne infection).

... but the distribution of the incidence of cases in the population is different

Flu pandemic of 1918

The "Spanish" flu was often referred to as the "largest medical holocaust in history". This not only because of the very high number of deaths caused by the infection, but also and above all because of the fact that most of the victims were young and in good health.

According to a hypothesis advanced to explain this observation, the H1N1 strain responsible for this influence had to hit the immune systems of these people in a particularly strong way, to trigger a cytochemical storm so intense as to flood the lungs of the infected subjects with fluids, obstructing the pathways respiratory areas.

It is likely that the elderly and children were spared from the most serious outcomes precisely because they are characterized by having a weaker immune system and, therefore, less reactive to infection.

Furthermore, it is hypothesized that the lower susceptibility to infection of both elderly people is due to having survived a flu strain very similar to that responsible for the pandemic, which spread in the human population in the 1930s.

New Coronavirus Pandemic
(SARS-CoV-2)

Older people and those with pre-existing diseases are considered to be at greater risk of meeting Covid-19, although the (very reduced) possibility that even young people may develop severe symptoms attributable to Covid-19 is not excluded.

In most cases, in young people and in the paediatric population, the disease presents with mild symptoms or is asymptomatic (although the latter condition does not limit its contagiousness).

The trend of the pandemic, in this case, seems to correlate with the gradual loss of efficiency of the immune system as the years go by and with the incomplete maturation of the same in paediatric age).

The dynamics of spreading the infection are also different in the two cases ...

The spread of the flu pandemic of 1918 had a slower trend than that of the new Coronavirus. An important role in these different dynamics of the spread of the two pandemics depends on the development of air mobility, still at the beginning in 1918. The "Spanish" influence spread mainly with rail and naval transport and was brought, according to some historians, by the troops who fought during the First World War.

... as well as living conditions and technological progress

In 1918 the pandemic was not known to be caused by a virus, so much so that the German bacteriologist Richard Pfeiffer had convinced almost all of the scientific community of the bacterial aetiology of the infection. It is only in 1933 that the viral origin of the infection will be demonstrated for the first time.

Antibiotics, capable of treating flu-related pneumonia (generally caused by bacteria) will only be discovered 10 years after the pandemic.

Antiviral drugs will be developed many years later than the 1918 flu pandemic (the first in 1963).

In 1918, the World Health Organization did not yet exist, a supranational body with one of its objectives to monitor the emergence of new diseases

Most European countries lived, in 1918, under censorship, with all the consequences of this situation (limited dissemination of accurate information on the flu epidemic, capable of saving lives).

What we learned from the experience of the 1918 flu pandemic and transferred to the management of pandemics of the future

1. Importance of the practice of "social distancing" and other non-pharmacological containment measures of the infection

Social distancing measures are today one of the main ways in which efforts are being made to contain the spread of the SARS-CoV-2 virus worldwide, after being applied first in China and in our country.

According to estimates from a report by the Imperial College of London, the adoption of these measures, together with those of home isolation and the total closure of non-essential activities, would have led to a reduction in the number of basic reproductions (R0) - or the average number of secondary infections produced by each infected individual in a population that never came into contact with the new emerging pathogen - below the unit, with an estimated 38,000 (IC95%: 13,000-84,000) deaths avoided for Covid-19 in our country and in the month of March just passed.

Not only that: a newly published study analysed the economic effects of the 1918 flu pandemic in US history, evaluating both the variation in the severity of the pandemic, as well as the timely application and duration of the non-pharmacological containment measures of the infection to combat the chain of contagions in American states and cities (closing of schools, theaters and places of worship, suspension of the celebration of weddings and funerals, quarantining of suspected cases and restriction of working hours).

Two important indications emerged from the analysis of the results:

- the area's most severely affected by the 2019 flu pandemic have experienced a strong and persistent decline in economic activities
- cities that promptly and extensively implemented non-drug containment practices of the infection did not suffer from adverse economic effects in the medium term.

Overall, therefore, the results of this study suggest that the pandemic may be associated with high economic costs but that the timely adoption of non-pharmacological infection containment measures could result in better economic scenarios, together with a reduction in mortality.

2. Importance of public health systems

At the time of the 1918 flu pandemic, states' expenditures were primarily directed towards military activities, while the public health system was still a necessity in embryo for most European countries.

At the time, the luxury of access to medical treatment was only possible for wealthy classes. For these reasons, the virus had an easy life in causing the death of a large part of the population living in disadvantaged urban areas, characterized by the absence of sanitation and malnutrition.

It will be necessary to wait until 1920, however, for the governments of the states that emerged from the first war conflict and a devastating pandemic to decide to move towards policies aimed at facilitating access to health care for the majority of the population.

Looking at the future

The adoption of measures of social distancing and, at the same time, the incessant work of doctors and researchers aimed at treating and finding solutions (drugs, vaccines) capable of slowing down the most harmful effects of pandemic infections and of breaking, by immunizing the population, the chain of infections, respond to the objective of treating pandemics as a collective problem and not exclusively of individual health.

But it is very much up to each of us to make sure that these efforts are crowned with success.

As mentioned, several times, nobody saves themselves!

Spanish flu and Coronavirus 100 years later

It was called Spanish flu or the great flu 100 years later still has something to teach

A century has passed since another great pandemic struck the world.

The epidemic broke out in the years of the First World War and the lack of hygiene, malnutrition and poverty facilitated the contagion.

The epidemic was called "Spanish flu" but not because it came from Spain, but because being this country out of the war, it had no censorship regarding information unlike other newspapers of the nations involved. From Spain then the news came and among the other the King himself fell ill with Spanish so it was inevitable to give the news.

The press of the other countries hid the severity of the Spanish flu and minimized the epidemic that between 1918 and 1920 killed about 50 million people, including 675,000 in the United States. He killed more than the plague of the fourteenth century and more than the Great War, of which it was in a certain sense the consequence.

Headache, muscle pain, tiredness, back pain, chills, dry cough, fever with temperatures above 40 ° C for a day or two. The disease lasted on average three, less often five or more days. Death usually occurred on the eighth or ninth day of illness, mainly due to secondary bacterial infection.

The most striking feature of the pandemic was its unusually high mortality rate among healthy people aged 15 to 34. Today it is believed that it was spread by American soldiers who had landed in

Europe since 1917 to take part in the Great War.

John M. Barry, author of the bestseller "The major influence" and a great connoisseur of the pandemic, has released an interview where the "The Listening Post" speaks of the similarities between L 'Spanish flu and Covid-19 and behavior of both the politics and the press.

The first accusation is directed at President Trump for hiding and giving contradictory information about the Coronavirus to the Americans, then talks about the press that hiding the news: "He made sure that things got worse, not telling the truth.

For example, a large rally was planned in the city of Philadelphia and the medical community warned that it was better to cancel the event and the publication of the news was prevented. Forty-eight hours after the flu incubation period, the disease exploded. The city was one of the hardest hits in the world.

In Wisconsin, when a newspaper tried to tell the truth about the pandemic, a lawsuit was launched against the publisher, for violating a law that included up to 20 years in prison. This was the initial attitude of the American government against anyone who wanted to tell the truth, "says John m. Barry, stressing the importance of information

When asked about the effects on the population at the news of the Spaniard, the author and scholar replies: " When there is an element of fear and you cannot believe what is being said, you can only rely on the voices you hear around, like the worst of the internet today.

One of the few cities where the authorities told the truth was San Francisco. A statute was published in local newspapers. Put on the mask and save your life now, it was written. It turned out that the masks didn't help. "

Four and a half million of infections and 600 thousand deaths on a population of 36 million inhabitants, the economy affected, social tensions, all between the Great War and fascism.

Yet we have very little memory or perhaps the memory today in the days of the Coronavirus is returning:

«Here the epidemic is continuously increasing; just look at the three columns of the dead of good people to be convinced of the mortality in the popular neighbourhoods. It is no longer known where to put the children orphaned by mothers and whose fathers are at the front. It is a problem to find doctors now.

Everyone is overwhelmed by work and basically nobody is cared for properly.

Perhaps the great mortality is also due to poor health care ".

A Fed and MIT study finds that during the Spanish flu pandemic in the United States alone there was an 18% drop in manufacturing production

According to some economists, in 1918 the cities that intervened first and with more restrictive measures to contain the contagion then experienced a more stable and lasting economic growth.

What can businesses learn from history?

While the hunger for liquidity continues to mark the business fabric and there is discussion about the sufficiency and the modalities of the measures put in place by the government, some economists have tried to place on the balance the current pandemic with the Spanish influence of

1918, in an attempt to offer a starting scenario in the post-covid shoot.

According to a study by the Federal Reserve and MIT's School of Management, Pandemic depress the economy, public health interventions do not: evidence from the 1918 flu, during the last century the Spanish flu pandemic caused over 50 million victims worldwide, affecting 0.66% of the American population.

There was only talk in the United States of a collapse in manufacturing production of 18%, with a growth in the insolvency of businesses and families.

Yet, the contagion containment measures, compared by scholars to those implemented in the current health context, showed positive effects in some cases. In particular, the cities that intervened earlier and with more restrictive measures would have been able to mitigate the negative effects of the pandemic, knowing then a more stable and long-lasting economic growth. But to what extent can a parallelism with the covid-19 pandemic really be made and what can businesses learn from history?

"There are three factors that make today's scenario different from that of the United States in 1918.

Firstly, today we are talking about a globalized economy. If at the time the effect of the pandemic on work and on the economy was fairly localized, today we suffer significant impacts from emergency management strategies by other countries and in the same way we transfer our strategies to them ".

In Germany, the automotive industry has been impacted by the management of phase 1, because an important supplier base resides precisely in the country. "The globalization of the supply chains is a driver that did not exist at the time and which today strongly affects the effect of pandemic management on the economy".

The second factor relates to infrastructure. There are a series of infrastructures that provide essential services for people, not relevant at the time of the Spanish influence, the existence of which could be jeopardized by lockdown measures since they have a certain level of rigidity and a low resilience in enduring periods of prolonged crises.

Finally, a final point to consider concerns the management of the infection. "We have knowledge and technologies that allow us to actively manage the pandemic and contain contagion even with a certain degree of social promiscuity, which did not happen then".

All factors that would make the current scenario "radically different", showing that today the strategies implemented in 1918 may not generate the same results.

A systemic approach to react to the crisis

Rather, a systemic approach is needed. "First of all because the crisis we are facing is an equally systemic crisis, which impacts directly on people and indirectly on all areas of social and economic life with which they interact.

This means guaranteeing an overall package of coherent measures both in terms of synergy and in terms of compensation.

So far this has been seen very little. " Secondly, we are moving towards an unknown scenario, "since a recovery of the activities in the company of covid will generate a different socio-economic structure than in the past, also for this reason we cannot draw a parallel with the Spanish influence of 1918".

Consequently, it is necessary "to be able to be adaptive in the set of measures that are proposed and put into practice, equipping themselves with punctual observation tools to re-evaluate our actions".

And on the issue of liquidity for businesses, the situation does not seem to be the best. "The fabric of our small and medium-sized enterprises works with liquidity at two months. We are now almost over the limits, and liquidity support measures have not yet largely reached the recipients ". In the medium term it will be necessary to focus on different financial actions. "We know that our SMEs suffer from chronic undercapitalization and at the moment it represents a huge vulnerability.

"We should support virtuous recapitalization actions or m & a operations for the consolidation of at least some strategic sectors in which, as a country, we express technological and market leadership.

We cannot allow covid-19 to wipe out these excellences. "

Conclusion - Possibility of future pandemic and how to prevent

The story of the epidemic that almost exactly a century ago killed between 50 and 100 million people worldwide.

During the First World War, the doctors of the large military hospital in Étaples, in the north of France, came across a respiratory disease with a particularly aggressive course. The affected patients, mostly young soldiers, were healthy in the morning and collapsed in bed in the evening, with blue lips from lack of oxygen.

In severe cases the symptoms of the disease included high fever, cough, nose and mouth bleeding, pneumonia and secondary pleurisy. Patients who did not end up killed by infections died suffocated in their beds.

The new disease was nicknamed "purulent bronchitis", since during the autopsy the bronchi of the patients were impregnated with infected liquid. The hospital doctors sent alarmed reports to their superiors, but with the high commanders engaged in the great offensives of 1916 and 1917, which cost hundreds of thousands of deaths, nobody paid much attention to them.

Then, as the front stabilized after the bloody losses of the previous months, the few outbreaks of the disease went out. And the soldiers in the hospitals returned to die of typhus and cholera, as before.

Purulent bronchitis, or a close relative of it, would soon return to visit not only the battlefields of Western Europe, but the whole world. In the spring of 1918 new outbreaks of a devastating haemorrhagic influence broke out in Étaples and then in the rest of France.

The epidemic spread rapidly to the German army, on the other side of the front, and arrived in the United Kingdom, beyond the English Channel. Facilitated by the movement of troops to the four corners of the world, the epidemic arrived in a few days in Italy, the United States, Russia, India and Africa. Most of the world was engaged in war and subjected to military censorship, while the only country where the epidemic and its effects could be freely discussed was Spain, where the disease had affected King Alfonso XIII among others.

In June 1918, newspapers thus began to speak of "Spanish flu", even though the new Spanish disease had very little. It was a global epidemic, the most devastating that mankind had ever seen. When the last wave ended, at the end of 1919, between 50 and 100 million people had been killed by the flu: a more devastating toll than that of the war just ended and a massacre at least equal in size to those of the Second World War which it would have erupted after twenty years.

The outbreak was of such size, and caused so many tragedies, that it is not unusual to see superlatives used to describe it. The historian Catharine Arnold, for example, called the Spanish epidemic "the greatest medical holocaust ever".

Arnold, a researcher at the University of Cambridge, is the author of 1918 Pandemic, the most recent of the numerous studies that have tried to answer the questions that scientists have been asking for over a century: what exactly was the Spanish flu epidemic, and why was it so lethal?

Arnold begins his story starting from the great progress made in recent years by a group of scientists, largely self-financed, engaged in finding out what exactly caused the pandemic. Starting in 2000, and often with enormous efforts, these scientists managed to recover enough infected material dating from the epidemic to sequence the genome of the responsible virus.

Their adventurous research included the exhumation of the bodies of some Inuit who died in Alaska in 1918 buried in permafrost and the removal of a sample of decayed fabrics from the lead coffin of Sir Mark Sykes, the British diplomat who died of flu in 1918 and gone down in history for the homonymous treatise.

Thanks to their work today we know that a flu virus A mutation (one of the four known types of flu, identified as A, B, C and D), belonging to the subtype H1N1 (the same that caused, in another mutation, was responsible for the 2009 swine flu pandemic).

Once the virus was identified, American scientists from the Centres for Disease Control (CDC) decided to rebuild it in order to study its effects. The experiment took place between huge safety devices. Only one doctor was authorized to conduct the job and only when the building had been abandoned by colleagues at the end of the shift.

The laboratory was accessible only by fingerprints and the freezer where the virus sample was stored could only be opened with a device that recognized the iris of his eye. Injected in some rats, the virus showed - a century after the epidemic - all its power. Some rats died in just three days and the virus proved to be a hundred times more lethal than the other strains of flu tested.

To describe the demonstrations of the destructive power of nature, American scientists have often resorted to epic tones: in front of their discovery, those of the CDC were no exception. The 1918 virus was "special", they wrote after observing its effects, "a mortal and unique product of nature, evolution and coexistence between animals and humans." A testimony to the "marvellous ability of nature to create pandemics".

The hundreds of episodes and individual experiences, often tragic and macabre, collected by Arnold in the four corners of the world and told in his book, do justice to the use of these biblical tones.

The British historian has reconstructed dozens of long-forgotten epidemic stories, obscured by the memory of the great tragedy of the First World War. Arnold, for example, tells of the terrible voyage of Leviathan, an American troop ship with 11,000 soldiers and sailors on board and left New York in September 1918. During the voyage to France on the ship an epidemic of Spanish influence broke out.

The doctors tried to contain the cases, but with each corridor of the ship crowded with cots and young soldiers, every effort was fruitless. In three days two thousand soldiers were sick in bed and the logbook described the corridors of the ship made slippery by "puddles of blood" due to the nasal bleeding of the sick. The bodies of 80 soldiers were thrown overboard before arrival in France and hundreds died in the following days.

Arnold tells how the first observers of the disease were surprised that, unlike normal epidemics, Spanish flu seemed to hit the healthiest and strongest people first. When the epidemic arrived in the United States, it found a perfect environment to spread: the long queues of boys queuing to enrol in the recruiting centres of their cities, intent on coughing and sneezing close to each other. In the spring of 1918, hospital beds - first along the east coast, then across the country - filled quickly.

A Chicago nurse's description of her hospital appears to come from a horror movie. The sick lay in bed, immobilized by the respiratory crisis, while the cyanotic color that their faces had assumed due to the lack of oxygen made it impossible to distinguish "whites from blacks". When their lungs collapsed, the air was trapped under the skin and bubbles could be felt by touching them with the hand. The moment had come to remove them from the beds, their bodies moved with the sheets "made the same crackling sound that you hear when pouring hot milk on puffed rice". Others had bleeding so strong that blood could splash from their nose to the other side of the room, and they had to get out of the way to avoid being hit.

The situation was so bad, says the nurse, that all the staff could do for the patients was to give them a glass of hot whiskey and then deal with the new cases that came to the ward. The dead piled up in the hundreds.

Further north, in Alaska, the epidemic made a silent massacre among the isolated indigenous communities, the same that scientists would have visited a century later in search of samples of the virus preserved by ice.

A group of fishermen ran into two undernourished and half-frozen children. Bringing them back to their village, they discovered that all the adults had been killed by the disease. In the isolated huts the inhabitants were found dead of cold because they were so sick that they were no longer able to keep the fire burning.

In June, the epidemic arrived in India, in Bombay, today Mumbai, at the time a British colony. The first sick to be identified were a group of policemen, some of whom worked at the port of the city, engaged in those hectic days to send troops, weapons and ammunition destined for the conflict. The colonial government blamed the Indians for poor sanitation, but local politicians and intellectuals accused the British authorities of their lack of interest in any health protection measure.

The Indians were right and the colonial government was wrong. Almost everywhere in the world, the infection began in the ports frequented by ships carrying Allied troops around the world. In Russia it began in the Arctic port of Archangel, where the allied convoys landed their supplies after circumnavigating the Scandinavian peninsula. In Iran the first outbreak was discovered in Shiraz, not far from the Persian Gulf, where British naval bases were based. The epidemic, facilitated by traditional pilgrims' movements within the country, caused a million deaths.

In Africa outbreaks broke out in ports along the route that led to India: in Tanzania, South Africa and Sierra Leone. While in the North of the continent the virus encountered a population that had already developed some form of immunity thanks to the epidemics of the past, the Spanish was the first great influence to visit Sub-Saharan Africa and dug in the population empty spaces that were filled only in the half century following. According to the largest estimates cited by Arnold, about 50 million people died in Africa.

In the meantime, Arnold writes, "the Spanish influence got what the German army had failed for four years": to conquer Europe. Between April and November, the whole continent was hit by two waves, and two less serious ones came the following year. In the UK, the disease began to manifest itself in the industrial cities of Northern England and overnight, whole factories found themselves with three quarters of the workers stuck at home by the disease.

Doctors suggested quarantine measures, but were often overlooked. The army fighting in Europe needed weapons and ammunition and the workers were asked to "hold on" and go to the factory even if they were sick. Eventually, two hundred thousand people would have died from the disease.

The psychosis of the epidemic spread rapidly in the country and people started to leave the house wearing heavy sanitary masks, while whiskey and scotch producers advertised their products as safe cures against the epidemic. On the front pages of newspapers, the Spanish influence was portrayed as a skeleton dressed as a flamenco dancer whose claws gripped Europe.

In Germany the disease, nicknamed "Blitz Katarrh", found a population weakened and prostrated by the famine that the allied naval blockade had imposed on the country. Over 400 thousand people were killed and the army chief of staff, General Erich Ludendorff, accused the epidemic of having failed his great 1918 offensive, with which he hoped to end the war once and for all. In Italy the epidemic broke out in the South and almost at the same time as the first cases occurred in French ports.

The reaction of the authorities, who had committed all the country's resources to the conflict with Austria-Hungary, was to ignore the problem. In particular in the South, therefore, the pandemic was faced with tragically inadequate medical means.

Over 600 thousand people died during 1918 and the subsequent waves of 1919, the most serious national budget on the continent. The historian of medicine Eugenia Toniotti recently dedicated a volume to this story, almost forgotten by national historiography, which has always been concentrated in the study of the First World War and on the advent of Fascism.

The horror of the deaths and the terror aroused by the epidemic and the violence of the contagion was made even more acute by the fact that not even the doctors knew what exactly was happening, and they had no means of fighting it. In 1918 doctors had never seen a "virus" with their eyes.

They only knew that there was a potentially deadly substance, but invisible to their tools. For some time, in fact, they had discovered that by filtering the infected water through an antibacterial filter, "something" still managed to pass through the very narrow pores. And that "something" was able to kill other bacteria beyond the filter.

Or possibly human cells. Doctors speculated that it was an enzyme or a tiny protozoan invisible to their optical microscopes. Without knowing what they were dealing with, they decided to call that substance "virus". Poison, in Latin.

When doctors in the spring of 1918 realized that what they had was an influenza epidemic, they knew that a "virus" was probably responsible, but they didn't know exactly what this meant or why the epidemic they faced was so lethal compared to the past. And the uncertainty, in a sense, still remains today that we know viruses much better (and, since the invention of the electron microscope in the 1930s, we have also begun to see them).

The H1N1 responsible for the pandemic, in fact, like all viruses, is located in a gray area between life and non-life. It is not really alive, but neither is it a completely inanimate substance. It can be considered at the same time a very complicated molecule, or the simplest of living beings.

H1N1, like all viruses, is essentially a piece of inert material: an RNA strand, which contains the information necessary to produce copies of itself, and a shell made of fats and proteins. But depending on how these proteins are arranged, a virus is able to penetrate the barriers of different types of cells from other organisms and, once inside, it is able to exploit the mechanisms of the cell to produce copies of itself. , sometimes killing the host in the process (although it is usually better for a virus to keep it alive and use it to spread other copies of itself).

The proteins that cover the H1N1 virus, like those of almost all influenza viruses, are of a type that allows it to penetrate the cells of the respiratory system: nasal mucous membranes, trachea, bronchi and lungs in particular.

After reproducing, the virus spreads through the microscopic aerosol particles emitted by speaking, breathing or coughing. This method of transmission is very effective and has allowed influenza viruses to be particularly successful. Another characteristic that distinguishes them is their high mutation capacity.

After having encountered a virus for the first time, in fact, the host's immune system is often able to recognize it and develop some form of defence. But if the virus changes between epidemic waves, the previously accumulated defences may be useless. It is a phenomenon that can be particularly serious when a virus "jumps" from one species to another that has no defence against the new variant. This species-jumping ability is present in numerous flu strains, which have been found in humans, birds and many mammal species.

Scientists have long been in agreement that all these factors have contributed to making Spanish flu particularly lethal.

Like most other hospitals around Europe, Étaples military hospital, the one where the first signs of the disease appeared in 1917, then exploded in 1918, was the perfect place to incubate a lethal virus. Built to accommodate the thousands of wounded from the fighting with the Germans, the camp consisted of an endless series of tents and shacks that extended to the horizon. This "smelly little town", as a witness called it, had beds for 20,000 patients and was served by ten thousand doctors and nurses.

Not far from the quarters there were stables for thousands of horses and fences for tens of thousands of chickens and pigs, slaughtered every day to feed the sick and passing troops: all animals known to host the flu virus.

The tons of animal excrements produced each month were then burned, in the absence of other methods to eliminate them, helping to wrap the field in an unhealthy yellowish haze, which worsened respiratory diseases and could help spread epidemics. There were also thousands of

Chinese workers in the camp, recruited in northern China to do non-military jobs.

Many of them came from an area of the country where a deadly flu epidemic that had killed thousands of people had developed just a few years earlier.

Incubated in a sort of gigantic virologic laboratory, the Spanish flu virus then found a perfect environment to spread. The movement of troops and civilians around the world due to the war allowed him to turn from a serious local epidemic into a global pandemic.

The weakness of millions of people subjected to the privations of war, the necessities of fighting, which prevented governments from concentrating the resources necessary to face the epidemic, and finally the opening up to communications of vast areas of the world once isolated, such as the African continent, which exposed millions of people to an infection they had never seen, did the rest.

A unique condition of factors made the Spanish flu epidemic the deadliest mankind had ever seen. But fortunately for us, such a complex combination of factors does not seem likely to come back for much longer.

The "great white plague" of 1918-19 caused 40 to 100 million deaths worldwide. That pandemic was called "Spanish" simply because, at the time, Spain, as a neutral country, was not subject to military censorship.

Therefore, unlike the belligerent countries, it could disseminate data and information. According to the most accredited historians, the first outbreak, which appeared in China (November 1917), then spread first to Canada and then to

Europe, following the Chinese workers (Chinese Labor Corps), implicated in the conflict by the Allies. A second, much more important, outbreak was formed shortly afterwards in the USA, in the military camp of Fort RIley (Kansas), with troops about to embark for Europe (August 1918), to participate in the final stages of the Great War.

These were young and healthy recruits who, before leaving, received numerous and repeated vaccinations "preventively" (typhoid / paratyphoid, yellow fever, etc.), which have now become mandatory practice in the US army since 1911.

Following these vaccinations, a "strange" surge in cases of typhoid syndromes, dozens of deaths, at least 20,000 hospitalizations in US military hospitals and almost 30,000 cases of hepatitis in just 6 months of war, resulted in the American army.

It is therefore probable that the combination between the two outbreaks (favoured by mass movements around the globe, together with the poor sanitation conditions in the trenches) and the suppression, induced by vaccinations, may have caused a genetic mutation of the virus, amplifying its virulence.

In fact, with the entry of the US into the war, both the civilians and the military involved in the conflict were quickly and seriously affected. Both the German and Austrian armies, for example, suffered heavy losses, when fortunes seemed to turn in their favour.

Not surprisingly, according to many scholars of medicine and military history, the Spanish decidedly changed the course of the war.

That "strange" epidemic took the entire academic community by surprise, which ignored its etiopathogenesis (the virus responsible was identified only in 1933 by a British team) and could offer simply symptomatic therapy, based exclusively on the vaccine, quinine and on salicylates.

Nevertheless, the mortality data in allopathically treated subjects were disastrous (20-40%) while in those treated with homeopathic therapy alone, mortality was around 1-2.1%.

According to the experience of European and American homeopaths, aspirin would have had a great responsibility in the fatal exit since its suppressive action would have given rise to serious pneumopathies in subjects already defected.

The successes reported by European and American homeopaths (which we intend to examine here), although never recognized by official institutions, are however evidenced by the choice of remedies and their case studies, from which an incredible concordance of data emerges.

Made in the USA
Monee, IL
23 August 2020

39385483R10069